W9-BUF-319

TODAY IN SCHOOL PSYCHOLOGY

This is why a day without direct contact with students is wasted

Charles A. Barrett

Today in School Psychology
This is Why a Day Without Direct Contact with Students is Wasted

Published by
CAB Publishing Company, LLC
PO Box 422
McLean, Virginia, 22101

ISBN-13: 978-1-7350264-0-4

CONTENTS

DEDICATION

To the children—
Thank you for inspiring me. Thank you for teaching me.
And even when I don't see you, I am always thinking about you.

ACKNOWLEDGMENTS

Although I believed in the message of *Today in School Psychology*, I wondered if it would be as meaningful to others as it was to me. Having known some of these amazing individuals for more than 20 years, I am grateful for their feedback that not only confirmed what I felt about the book, but also motivated me to finish it. I am honored to consider them colleagues and friends.

Jessica Anderson
School Psychologist Intern
Bellevue School District

Amber Boykin, SSP, NCSP
School Psychologist
Lincoln Parish Schools

Dwayne Bryant, PhD, NCSP
School Psychologist
Evergreen Elementary School District

Christina Conolly, PsyD, NCSP
Director of Psychological Services
Montgomery County Public Schools

Brit Cooper, EdS
Mental Health Specialist
Lewis County Schools

Rio Corbin, EdS, NCSP
School Psychologist
Independence School District

Dywane Dawkins, Sr., MA
Teacher, Charter Schools USA
Lead Pastor, Praise Tabernacle International

Eric Elias, MSEd, ABSNP
School Psychologist
Meriden Public Schools

Barbara Fromal, MEd
Eligibility Coordinator
Loudoun County Public Schools

Beth Lanthier, PhD
Professor of Psychology
Northern Virginia Community College

Danielle Guttman-Lapin, PhD, NCSP

Byron McClure, DEd, NCSP
Student Redesign Experience Coach
District of Columbia Public Schools

Chelsea McDowell, EdS, NCSP
School Psychologist
North Kansas City Schools

Tim McIvor, CAGS, NCSP
School Psychologist
Marion County Public Schools

Em Meyer, EdS
School Psychologist Intern
Independence School District

Aline Milfort, MS
Graduate Student
Nova Southeastern University

Rosalyn Pitts Clark, PhD
School Psychologist
Atlanta Public Schools

Byron Preston, MM
Teacher, Center Moriches School District
Pastor, Life Empowerment Worship Center Long Island

Sherrie Proctor, PhD
Associate Professor of School Psychology
Queens College, City University of New York

Colin Reiley, MEd
Teacher
Loudoun County Public Schools

Kelly Shanks, SSP, NCSP
School Counselor
Sacred Heart Academy

ABOUT TODAY IN SCHOOL PSYCHOLOGY

When speaking to educators and various parent and community groups, I often share a few short stories about my interactions with the students in my schools. More than the smiles (and maybe laughter) from the audience, these brief moments allow them to understand who I am as a person and how I think as a school psychologist. Perhaps best described as a diary, *Today in School Psychology: This is Why a Day Without Direct Contact with Students is Wasted* includes some of my encounters with children and musings on school psychology and education.

Most of the entries in this collection were written at the end of day while thinking about how amazing it is to be a school psychologist. From being incredibly proud of students who have graduated from high school to highlighting the outstanding families and colleagues who passionately serve and advocate for young people, this book has something for you.

Most of all, *Today in School Psychology* is filled with the innocence and insight of children. Whether using the anecdotes as icebreakers or discussion starters during staff meetings and retreats, or enjoying them for personal inspiration, I hope that *Today in School Psychology* encourages you to become an even better champion for young people—one who always keeps children at the center of their service and professional practice.

CAB

GRADUATION DAY

I am extremely proud of the Park View High School Class of 2017! Although graduation was great, once again, I had mixed emotions. Seeing some of these outstanding young people walk across the stage to receive their diplomas—some as the first person in their families—was nothing short of amazing. For one student, I literally saw her walk for the first time. I really have the best job in the world. Having known and worked with some of these young people since 4th grade, I've witnessed their hard work, focus, and relentless determination to succeed in spite of challenging circumstances, significant adversity, and what others said they could not achieve. In the words of Michael Vereb, "I love you and I'm proud of you."

SUMMER VACATION

While spending the last ten days vacationing with Lisa and Miles, I couldn't help but think of all the boys and girls whose families can't afford this privilege. I'm especially grateful that we have jobs that allow us time away without penalty. It could be otherwise, and it is for too many families. Improving students' achievement is not only about more or better instruction in reading, writing, and arithmetic; equally important to their development are rich experiences beyond their communities that expand their perspective and exposure. Because it's always about the children, looking forward to the day when these opportunities and experiences are accessible to all.

FIRST DAY OF SCHOOL

Tomorrow is the first day of school and I'm just as excited as I was when I was a child packing my backpack and supplies. When I no longer feel this way about the first day, and saddened by the last day, is the day that I need to find something else to do.

SCHOOL PSYCHOLOGY AWARENESS WEEK

Earlier today I attended a meeting to discuss a student's academic difficulties. Although her parents disagreed with our recommendation to evaluate the student, it was a great meeting. The parents, immigrants who speak Arabic, Somali, and English, are fierce advocates for their daughter. In sum, they weren't comfortable with the possibility of their daughter being a child with a disability. I respect their position. At times it's hard enough identifying students with disabilities; I have no idea how this feels for a parent. In sum, our conversation was a respectful dialogue of differing opinions that was centered on the student's success. Although I felt strongly about the student's academic difficulties, because the parents were listened to, and their perspective was valued, I left the meeting pleased with the outcome. Morals of the story:

1. Our views aren't the only important ideas to consider.
2. Parents' perspectives and being comfortable with the direction of their children's education are of utmost importance.
3. If parents, or other team members, disagree with our analysis, it's okay.

IEP MEETING

Earlier today I attended an Individualized Education Plan (IEP) meeting to support a friend and her son. As I listened to the input from the teachers, social worker, school counselor, and assistant principal, I was pleased with what they said and the manner in which they respected the student and his family. I was particularly impressed with the school psychologist and her contributions. After the meeting, I let her know that she did a great job and that I was also a school psychologist. It was a pleasure to see a colleague in action—serving students and families with sensitivity. Moral of the story: we never know who's watching what we're doing. There are people who attend our meetings who know at least as much as we do. Serve. Always.

CLASSROOM OBSERVATIONS

I spent some time observing students in five classrooms today at Forest Grove Elementary School and Guilford Elementary School. I always enjoy seeing great instruction and active student engagement! There's nothing like serving with committed educators in public schools.

GUITAR PRACTICE

One of my students asked me to come to his guitar practice this afternoon. He and the other students were great! Because I enjoy it so much, I can't call it a job. I absolutely love what I do each day.

"HE'S BLACK!"

As I was preparing to evaluate a student, a
5-year-old Black child pointed at me and exclaimed,
"He's Black!" Notably, I wasn't in one of my
assigned schools, but a portion of the county that
is considerably less diverse. When this happened,
I couldn't help but wonder if this student had
ever seen a Black male in a professional position.
Would he ever have the experience of a Black, male
teacher? While the surprise and excitement from his
voice made my day, it also renewed my commitment
to diversifying the field of school psychology. I
shouldn't be an anomaly.

KEVIN MCCALLISTER

My day began with evaluating a 1st grade student. During a memory span subtest, instead of waiting for me to finish saying a string of numbers, he was trying to say them with me. To redirect his response style, I said, "Wait until I'm done [insert student's name]." His response? "Wait until I'm done [insert student's name]." Although he was in 1st grade, he knew exactly what he was doing. Admittedly, he made me laugh, which he enjoyed as well. I felt like I was working with Kevin McAllister. As much as I may have been trying to understand this youngster's cognitive functioning, he reminded me that a day without direct contact with a student is wasted.

FOR THE CULTURE

Highlight of the day: talking to a young brother about his locks.

DEAR SCHOOL PSYCHOLOGIST

If we spend twice as much time listening as we do speaking, we'll be more effective. Enjoyed spending my morning with teachers at two very different schools addressing very different situations. Grateful that I learned a lot in the process.

SUMMER SLIDE

As a musician, my only regret is that I never disciplined myself to read music more fluently. Every so often I am reminded of this limitation when I'm in a situation in which reading fluently would make life easier. As a school psychologist, I've been thinking of the similarities between reading music and children's literacy. Especially as we approach the end of the school year, the summer slide is a real phenomenon. In other words, students, especially developing and struggling readers, return to school in the fall reading at lower levels than they were at the end of the previous school year. Why? In a lot of ways, lack of practice. When I was consistently reading music, even for only 20 minutes each day, I was much better at it. Similarly, when students read every day, they grow. When they're not, especially over the summer... What can we do to pool resources to ensure that students have sufficient reading materials and support to continue reading for 20 minutes each day, which will prevent the summer slide?

MUST BE THE BIRTHDATE

For the first time, I evaluated a student with whom I share a birthday. While writing his birthdate, it occurred to me that I am exactly 24 years older than he is. He was a laid back, yet very hardworking young man. He did well. Must be the birthdate.

A PLAY-DOH TOWER

I was hanging out with a 3rd grade friend last week. Between working on his assignments, he played with Play-Doh. I saw this on my desk after asking him to clean up a few things he was using. I asked him about it, and he thought it was quite funny. He was right. If you can't work with a student every day, you can certainly smile about one. Happy Monday!

PLAY-DOH MAKES EVERYTHING BETTER

One of my kindergarten friends was working in my room today. We talked about focusing on the good things that he does. After showing him my collection of Sharpie markers that he could use to circle the points on his behavior plan, I saw this on my desk.

Lesson #1: All children have strengths and can do something well.
Lesson #2: Play-Doh makes everything better.

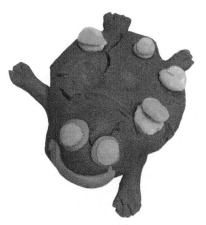

DEFINITION OF A TEACHER

teach·er (n.)

: special people who take care of other people's children as if they were their own.

I began my day with two Forest Grove Elementary School teachers who gracefully embody this sentiment. Thanks Ms. McKinney and Mrs. Robles for showing that it's always about the children.

A FRIEND FOR MR. FROG

Happy Friday.

REALLY, I DO

If I didn't write another report for the rest of the school year, I really would be okay.

I love my job—really, I do. I love to write—really, I do. And most of all, I love the children whom I serve—really, I do. However, there comes a point in every school year when writing reports gets to be my favorite activity to avoid. Having already evaluated students through July, guess what I'll be doing for the next several weeks.

BACK TO SCHOOL EVE

The moment that I am no longer excited about the first day of school is the day that I will no longer be a school psychologist.

Because tomorrow is the first day of school, I think that I'll return to my today in school psychology posts. Having been assigned a new school this year, over the past two days I've been reacquainted with two individuals that I haven't seen or worked with in several years. Both parents, one is also a staff member at my new school. I'm glad that seeing them again wasn't awkward because I didn't treat them or their children with the utmost respect. Said another way, we can be remembered for being exceptionally good to children and families or... And for my friends in graduate school or entering the profession, school psychology is an extremely small world. Everyone knows someone. Serve. Always.

ASSUMPTIONS

All parents want the best for their children.

While watching parents and families bring their children to school this morning, I was reminded of these words by one of my practicum supervisors: until we know otherwise, assume that all parents want the best for their children. Regardless of race, ethnicity, gender, income, and a host of other differences, I saw the same excitement and optimism in the faces of all families who entrusted their children to educators whom they believe also want the best for their students. If we have to assume, let's assume the best in others.

RELATIONSHIPS MATTER

Good teachers not only cultivate relationships with their students, but they facilitate a healthy classroom community by encouraging their students to develop relationships with each other.

Loved seeing and hearing 5th grade students compliment each other and creatively learn about their classmates. Outstanding job, Jill Redenburg!

HOW OLD ARE YOU?

"How old are you?"
"Eight. How old are you?"
"A lot older than eight."

A conversation with a youngster I was
working with earlier today. Happy Friday.

SEEING IS BELIEVING

I began my day in the 3rd grade classroom of my friend, Suzanne Elbeze. She told the students that I wrote a book, which led to many questions about writing books. As much as I loved their excitement and interest, and enjoyed answering their questions, more importantly I hope that these youngsters, most of whom represented culturally and linguistically diverse backgrounds, were inspired to write their own books having seen and known someone who looks like them do the same.

STUTTERING

Over time I've learned that stuttering was not an impediment or stumbling block, but a steppingstone...

This morning I was a guest reader for a local school's *One Book, One School event*. I'm sharing this to encourage those who may live with disabilities or other weaknesses that are beyond their control. As a child, I had a rather significant stutter and participated in school-based speech therapy for six years. Being recorded reading was something that I would have never volunteered to do as a youngster. At times, speaking in class or knowing that I would have to read aloud was quite nerve wracking. Perhaps this is why I prefer listening rather than speaking. Perhaps this is why I prefer writing or expressing myself through music... I want to encourage you: never allow anything to silence your voice. Especially for children who may stutter or live with other speech impediments, what you have to say is important. Lesson: allow the things that try to slow you down inspire you to be better and achieve your goals.

LISTEN TO CHILDREN

Spent some time with a young brother. A 2nd grader, he repeatedly told me that he was mad. While I was trying to understand why he was so upset, including being mad at me, eventually it became clear: I wasn't understanding what he was saying. Although he felt that he was being perfectly clear with me about what was bothering him, it took me longer than he felt it should have to get what he was saying. In his frustration, he left the room and wandered throughout the school. After almost an hour of walking around the building, turning his back to me, ignoring me, and raising his voice, I understood what he was saying. After he knew that I understood him, almost immediately, he shook my hand, allowed me to tie his shoes, and was ready to return to class. He didn't want me to fix anything. He simply wanted to be heard. He wanted to be understood.

"YOU ARE BIG AND BROWN AND HAVE BROWN SKIN."

I was evaluating a 6-year-old student this morning who was absolutely delightful. His energy and enthusiasm throughout the session reinforced why I became a school psychologist—to serve children. At some point during Word Definitions, he told me this: "You are big and brown and have brown skin." As always, the innocence of children makes me smile. Food for thought: if children see color, why do some adults insist that they don't? After all, the problem isn't that we see color; it's what we make ourselves see—that really isn't there, but a remnant of how we've been taught to view others—in those of different colors.

MY WHOLE SELF

I know that I am doing what I was created to do because I can bring my whole self to what I do.

I stopped in to see Mrs. Redenburg's 5th grade class—some of the coolest students I know! They were working on writing introductory paragraphs. She told them that I was an author and they had many questions! "What's your book? How much is it? Is it on Amazon?" I showed them a picture of the book on my phone and some said that it looked like a children's book or what a kid would pick up. The children are honest! I told them that to be a good writer you have to read and practice writing. Grateful that my passions intersect and that I can bring my whole self to what I do each day.

FORREST GUMP

One of my favorite movies is *Forrest Gump*[1]. Although I've seen it numerous times, while driving earlier today, I thought about something for the first time. There's a scene in which a school official (I'm pretty sure Mr. Haycock is the principal) shows Mrs. Gump (Forrest's mother) where he scored on an IQ test. Further, because it was below 80, he would not be allowed to attend public school. Mrs. Gump, not willing to accept this answer, and in the words of Forrest, wanting him to "...have the finest education..." replied, "...He's not going to some special school to learn how to re-tread tires...!" A few things:

1. Parents and families often know their children better than professionals think they do.
2. IQ tests never tell the complete story of who children are—especially who they are capable of becoming and what they are capable of accomplishing.
3. In the words of one of my Howard University graduate students, "not all IQ tests are created equal." Maybe the school psychologist administered the wrong/less valid test to young Forrest.
4. Parents and families can be their children's most effective advocates.

As the movie unfolds, although Forrest may have performed below normative expectations on an IQ test, he was gifted in other ways. Lesson: every child is gifted. As educators and guardians, it is our job to help them identify their gifts. For Forrest, it was running. His speed could not be taught or developed through practice alone. And as he began to use his gift, it opened numerous opportunities for him that changed his life—and the course of history.

[1]Zemeckis, Robert, director. *Forrest Gump*. Paramount Pictures, 1994.

DEAR EDUCATOR

Your student is someone's child.

Started the day reading some amazing report card comments by an outstanding teacher! The student was no longer in her class, but what she said was tremendously helpful for my understanding of the student. I admired how she framed the student's difficulties in a way that was both positive and respectful. The words that we use to describe students matter to their families.

AN ENDORSEMENT AND A HUG

"I think you'll have fun with my friend."
"Can I give you a hug?"

While preparing to work with a student, he saw a friend in the hallway. The friend, a 2nd grade student that I had previously worked with, said that he (his friend) would have fun with me. Because children only tell the truth (smile), when they tell their friends that they'll have fun with you, it must be! Thanks for the endorsement and compliment, young man!

And when I was getting into my car, a 1st grade student that I worked with earlier this school year was walking with his mother. After I said hello, he came over and gave me a hug.

UNCONDITIONAL POSITIVE REGARD

As educators, we must show our students that   we value and care about them as individuals and not based on their academic performance. Mr. Huey at Countryside Elementary School is an outstanding teacher who consistently exemplifies that it's always about the children.

FACT AND TRUTH

Justice includes finding the truth about students. While facts may tell us what they cannot do, this may not be the truth of who they are and all that they can accomplish.

While administering a Fluid Reasoning task to a 1st grader, I learned a lot from the young man as he verbalized his thought process. He said things such as: "AABB" or "ABAB" or "ABCABC." The student clearly knew that the task involved identifying patterns and was applying a strategy that he had been taught [in school]. While such thinking/reasoning enabled him to earn a score that fell within the Average range, his behavior further confirmed my growing concerns about the nature of cognitive ability assessments. Essentially, are they truly measuring students' ability to think/reason? Or, are they confounded by academic achievement and what students have been exposed to instructionally? What do you think?

March 3, 2019

THANK YOU

...We met during your workshop on Wednesday and the meet and greet Thursday morning. The reason for this email is twofold. I wanted to thank you for your kind, inspirational, and motivating message and passing along your book. Further, I wanted to thank leaders like you and Dr. Celeste Malone for your advocacy and motivating students like myself to gain/have a voice within the field... Having the outlet within NASP and resources you leaders have revealed will undoubtedly help myself (and many others). In essence, thank you for being the model and role model I sought as a working professional, advocate, and educator.

Without a doubt, meeting and engaging with graduate students, especially those from diverse backgrounds, is the most exciting and fulfilling part of any National Association of School Psychologists (NASP) Convention, state association conference, or professional gathering. I received this note a few days ago and am absolutely grateful to have met this young man. Like the students I serve each day, more than what I may have imparted to him, he gave me so much more. Being on the other side of graduate school, I can relate to some of what he wrote. For a long time, Rosalyn Pitts Clark was the only Black school psychologist that I knew. Quincy Jones says it this way: "You want to be what you see." I continue to be encouraged and inspired by the young people I meet who are persevering through challenging situations to achieve their goals. Their commitment, drive, and dedication are nothing short of amazing and outstanding. Young brother, young sister, I see you. Keep pushing. You'll make it. The field needs your voice and your presence.

JUSTICE IS ABOUT ACCESS

For parents and families, schools that are committed to ensuring justice and equitable outcomes for all students intentionally provide parents with the necessary information and resources so that they are equipped to be the most informed advocates for their children.

During a meeting earlier today, I was reminded of the far-reaching implications of social justice in schools. As a parent was advocating for what she felt was best for her child, it became apparent that a lot of her frustration with the system was the result of how she was treated several years ago by school staff. While they likely did not mean to overlook her concerns, how she felt today was the result of what did not happen for her child. I remain convinced that more than our technical competencies in various disciplines, families want us to first validate their concerns and explain what is happening with their child in terms that are understandable. In fact, the ability to explain complex information in a way that is clear to laypersons shows that we truly know what we're doing and talking about. Being patient with families goes a long way. Not knowing their past experiences, we may also need to restore their trust in the process and the system. Thanks to some wonderful colleagues for how they listened to a concerned parent and explained things in ways that were meaningful and helpful. It's okay to disagree, but only after we've given families an opportunity to share their thoughts and feelings about their children.

March 27, 2019

"YOU'RE REALLY NICE."

A 4th grade student told me this earlier today. It reminded me of what a teacher, Linda Eberle, told me while I was completing a practicum at James Rhoads Elementary School in Philadelphia 15 years ago: children know your heart. Thank you, young man.

"DO YOU KNOW MY NAME?"

Whenever I'm in kindergarten or 1st grade classrooms, students often excitedly ask me: "Do you know my name?" Fundamentally, this simple question shows that children want to know that they are seen and valued as individuals. As educators, knowing our students by name and correctly calling them by their names goes a long way.

CATS AND CODING

Be happy with those who are happy, and weep with those who weep[2].

Sometimes school psychology is sitting with a student who lost the pet he's known his entire life and listening to him talk about how much he loves coding.

---

[2]*Be happy with those who are happy, and weep with those who weep*. Romans 12:15. The Holy Bible, New Living Translation. Copyright © 1996, 2004, 2007 by Tyndale House Foundation. Used by permission of Tyndale House Publishers, Inc., Carol Stream, Illinois 60188. All rights reserved.

FAMILIES AREN'T ARGUING, THEY'RE ADVOCATING

It's okay to disagree with families about the best course of action for a child if you have truly listened to and valued their perspective.

Fundamentally, parents and educators won't always agree on the most appropriate course of action for a student; and that's okay. Today I'm grateful for serving with colleagues who valued listening to parents, respected their perspective, and respectfully disagreed with their wishes. Because how we do things is often as important, or even more important than what we do, the manner in which the discussion unfolded enabled the family to leave the meeting feeling heard, valued, and genuinely respected. It can be done.

NOT AIR GUITAR, BUT AIR DRAWING

You've likely heard about air guitar, but have you ever seen a child air draw?

After co-facilitating a professional learning session focused on equity, I went to a school and evaluated a 5th grade student. While administering a visual memory subtest, the student drew the pictures in the air before transferring them to paper. It was his strategy. A simple approach, but it worked. I really enjoyed watching him put forth such concerted effort to do well. While it's not always possible, this is why a day without direct contact with a child is wasted.

ADVICE FROM A 5TH GRADER

**"It'll be cool for the alphabet book if teachers
read it for Black History Month."**

After almost 11 years, it's hard for me to say
that school psychology is my job because it never
feels like work. Today began by spending about an
hour with two absolutely delightful 5th graders who
had an interest in becoming authors. They asked
excellent and insightful questions about how they
could become writers and they let me read a few of
their pieces. It was great to see their faces light up
with excitement. I showed them the three books that
I've written so far, and one student said that he'd
seen *It's Always About the Children*[3] somewhere
(but not at school). They asked if I was working on
anything and I told them about a book that Lisa and
I were writing. The quote above is what one student
said about the forthcoming book. As much as I may
have helped them learn about becoming authors,
they were so much more encouraging, inspiring,
and interested in a book about social justice. At

[3]Barret, Charles A. *It's Always About the Children*. CAB Publishing Company, 2018

the end, the young man asked for a copy of *It's Always About the Children*. It was a pleasure to sign them and speak into their lives. Of all the books I've signed, without a doubt, these are the most special. Thanks to Alysia Brown, school counselor at Forest Grove Elementary School, for envisioning and planning such a wonderful unit to expose students to what they can and will accomplish.

"WHAT'S UP WITH YOU BARRETT?"

Spent a few hours evaluating two students that I've known for at least one year. They are very different children with strong, yet absolutely delightful personalities. While walking in the hallway with the 2nd grader, I was looking for a pen in my jacket's inside pocket. Because of who he is, his question was amusing and not at all disrespectful. And although I don't prefer it, he's probably the only child who almost always calls me Dr. Barrett. Especially in May, amidst evaluations and a host of other responsibilities, this is exactly why a day without direct contact with students is wasted.

"I DON'T KNOW HOW TO."

As we begin another day, remember these words from a 5th grader I was evaluating a few days ago. We were walking to his classroom and his shoes were untied. I suggested that he tie them so that he wouldn't fall. Very simply, he said these words. And guess what happened? I tied them for him. Sometimes help is on the other side of acknowledging what we don't know.

May 9, 2019

EVEN IF THEY AREN'T MY STUDENTS...

I had the pleasure of listening to some of the most intelligent and socially conscious young people I've ever met. Thanks to Mary Cohen and Jill Snyder for allowing Ivonne Borrero, Todd Savage, and I to speak to students at Another Course to College (ACC) in Hyde Park, Massachusetts! But more than sharing with them about the field, it was inspiring to hear them talk candidly about their perceptions of what school psychologists should do to better support students. At the core of their comments was the importance of connecting to students, talking to everyone, and having more school psychologists—especially those from diverse backgrounds. Kudos to their outstanding principal, Michele Pellam, and school psychologist, Shanice Hines, who has already made an indelible impact on these students in one year! We can really learn a lot when we listen to children. This is why a day without direct contact with students (even if they aren't my students) is wasted.

LISTEN TO FAMILIES

They are experts in their children.

Dear School Psychologist—

I was reminded of this truth earlier today. I recently
evaluated a student who had interrupted education.
Without sharing the details, and through no fault
of her own, she missed an entire year of school.
After a series of pre-referral meetings, the school-
based team did not suspect that the student had
an educational disability. Her mother, however,
strongly disagreed and continued to advocate for
her child and what she felt was in her best interest.
After assessing the student's cognitive abilities
and academic skills, it was rather evident that a
Specific Learning Disability was likely contributing
to the student's academic underachievement.

Lessons:

1. As educators and professionals, we can be wrong.
2. Listen to families. We may be experts in our respective disciplines, but they are bonafide experts in their children.
3. Families: never stop advocating for your children.

"COMPUTER IS GOING CRAZY."

Confession: I am questioning whether assessing Crystallized Intelligence (Gc) provides meaningful information to predict children's academic achievement. Because race and culture matter, while assessing a monolingual, 3rd grade, White student, this was his response to a Gc item. For obvious reasons, I won't share the name of the instrument or the exact question; however, his response, in my opinion, was not incorrect. If anything, it represented an understanding of the word based on children's contemporary access to, and familiarity with, computers and other forms of technology. Unfortunately, based on the technical manual, the response was scored as incorrect.

Was that fair to the student? This could be another example of the fact that in most cases the children are fine; it's the big kids (e.g., in this case test developers) around them who may need more help. While knowing what words mean is important, is it a cognitive ability? The more I practice, the more convinced I become that it's really achievement—learned information—masquerading as ability. Especially if the goal of assessment is to inform intervention recommendations, we must be sure that we are indeed measuring constructs that are worth our time—and children's effort—because they are significantly related to positive outcomes for children.

June 3, 2019

"WHAT ARE YOU DOING HERE?"

While completing my last classroom observation of the school year, a kindergartner asked me this question. Children have a way of telling you exactly what is on their minds (smile). After asking the teacher about another student that we were concerned about earlier in the year, she confirmed that it was the same youngster who asked me why I was in his classroom. He was doing great and read an entire list of sight words to me. Sometimes children simply need the gift of time. Great job, teacher! His mother also didn't give up on him. Great job, mother! And most of all, great job, young man!

A 13-YEAR-OLD'S PERSPECTIVE ON PURPOSE

"Something you're meant for."

June 6, 2019

[WITH A BIG SMILE], "HEY! I HAVEN'T SEEN YOU IN A LONG TIME!"

Today, on the eve of the last day of school, I saw this young brother in the hallway. To say that he was in a much better mood would be an understatement. I also saw him throughout the year, and he was usually very pleasant. Today, however, he seemed really happy. I love to see children happy[4].

[4]See October 18, 2018.

FAMILY FORUM

At the end of the day, I had the best and most unique meeting with a family. Originally scheduled to discuss autism spectrum disorder with a father who wasn't able to attend his son's recent eligibility meeting, the student's mother and sisters (ages 11 and 19) also came. Having started the meeting with the father, when the mother arrived, I asked if she wanted her children to be in the room. She said yes. I must say: having never been in this situation before, it was absolutely beautiful. Although there were concerns that the father may have some difficulty accepting his son's disability classification, he did not. But more than that, it was a dynamic discussion about how they—as a family—could help their son and brother with his social and behavioral weaknesses. Each family member knew their son and brother intimately. The sisters were genuinely interested and asked detailed and insightful questions. And guess what? The 19-year-old young lady took Advanced Placement (AP) psychology in high school and was familiar with... school psychology! She's going to email me about the profession. She'll be a great school psychologist! At the end, the mother was also relieved that she hadn't done anything to cause her son to have autism. Thanks to Belinda (Bella) Cermola, an outstanding interpreter, who facilitated such a productive and effective discussion.

June 7, 2019

ANOTHER YEAR OVER, AND A NEW ONE'S JUST BEGUN[5].

Confession: the last day of school is always a sad day for me. Yes, breaks are healthy and necessary; that's why we have snow days. Happy Summer to all of the children and families of Loudoun County Public Schools.

[5]Lennon, John and Ono, Yoko. "Happy Christmas."
This is Christmas, Apple Records, 1971.

CLASS OF 2019

While graduation teaches us that hard work pays off, commencement signals new beginnings and boundless possibilities. Be encouraged, graduate!

Congratulations to the Park View High School Class of 2019! While every class is special, these young people are different for too many reasons. The first student that I worked with in Loudoun County Public Schools (LCPS) graduated today. To say that he has come a long way since I met him as a rising 1st grader is an understatement. Another graduate and I used to walk [outside] around the school because this was calming for him. When he saw me, he said, "I'm better now." A young lady has an incredibly bright future as she pursues child development. From our conversations over the past two years, I was honored that she and her mother trusted me to listen to what was on her mind and speak into her life. I could never put into words what these young people mean to me. My nine years at Park View High School will always be some of the

nost special days of my life. Although you're not
:hildren anymore, I will never forget when I met
:ach of you—some as much as 11 years ago—and
.he joy you've given me to witness your growth and
naturity. I'm proud of you.

SAY MY NAME?

[child's name] is doing well with regulating his behaviors and completing assignments on time. [gender] is experiencing difficulty regulating his emotions and requires teacher prompting and support to complete assignments on time.

While it's not always possible, whenever I'm describing students' positive attributes, I try to say/write their names. However, when I'm discussing their weaknesses, I am more inclined to use their gender. Albeit subtle, it's my intentional way of associating as much positivity as possible to their names. I think parents appreciate hearing good news with their children's names rather than the not-so-positive information that we must also share. For families, it's the little things, that turn out to be big things, that really count.

DISAGREEING WITHOUT BEING DISAGREEABLE

We can disagree without being disagreeable.
Contentious meetings are often the
result of one party who refuses to listen
more than they are speaking.

Being a part of eligibility team meetings to help
determine if a student has an educational disability
is never easy. Despite some situations being clearer
than others, it's never something that I take lightly.
During a recent meeting with a parent, the more I
listened to her, the better I understood what she was
(and was not) feeling and communicating about her
son. Ultimately, she was deeply concerned about his
well-being. Like any other family, she wanted what
was in his best interest. After carefully discussing
various eligibility categories, we determined that
the student did not have an educational disability;
however, there are legitimate concerns and they will
be addressed through other creative mechanisms.
I appreciated the respectful tone that was present

throughout the meeting and the staff's ability to ask questions and listen to a mother who was advocating for her child. In fact, it reinforced the importance of not only being mindful of what we say, but also how and when we say certain things to families. If we listen twice as much as we speak, we will reach a resolution that values everyone's perspective. Thanks to Shanna Takacs for facilitating a very productive meeting.

August 21, 2019

DEAR DR. BARRETT

When I first read your kind words back in
June, I was overwhelmed with emotions that a
simple thank you would not do! Sorry for waiting too
long to gather my thoughts. [student] has come a
long way due to the attention of a professional panel,
a caring teacher and loving parents. But I do want to
thank you for taking the time to observe [student]
and sharing your observation and suggestions with
me. Also, for having a one-on-one chat with me that
one time, it helped me so much. Thank you again for
your kindness!

It's always a pleasure receiving notes like this
from parents and families. On this Back to School
Eve, I am even more committed to serving students,
families, schools, and communities. Listening to
families and teachers will always be time well spent.

I'M TELLING THE TEACHER

Teachers are amazing individuals.
It's not always easy caring for many children—each
with a unique story and history. When teachers do
this well, it's imperative that we let them know how
much they're appreciated.

Much respect to Margaret Ayers and the other
educators who take care of other people's children
as if they were their own by understanding the
immeasurable value of listening to families.

I'M A GOOD KID

"I want to brag more... because I'm a good kid."

I was writing a report and heard, "He's here!" from the hallway. One of my 5th grade friends excitedly came into the room with his teacher because he was having an amazing day and wanted to brag. To see the pure joy on his face was absolutely inspiring. I enjoyed seeing him smile as his teacher took the time to tell me about three instances in which he made great choices to manage his emotions. Having known he and his family for many years, this was indeed great to see and hear. The quotes above are his words. He was proud of himself and I am proud of him, too.

October 2, 2019

MUSIC TO MY EARS

"My mom never told me what a --- is."

Evaluated two students and they taught me a lot. I thoroughly enjoyed hearing one student (2nd grade) verbalize her thought process while solving various items across subtests. The second student (1st grade) said some of the simplest, yet profound words about the cognitive abilities that we assess. Both of them reminded me of a quote by Jack Naglieri. While one child confirmed for me what the essence of intelligence is—the ability to think, reason, and solve problems—the other's response to a question assessing Crystallized Intelligence (i.e., background knowledge) underscored that this ability is really achievement or a skill that must be taught. If we continue to conflate intelligence with culturally specific factual knowledge or vocabulary, we will do our students—and some more than others—not only a disservice, but an injustice. This is why a day without direct contact with a student is wasted.

74

Today in School Psychology

"HEY BARRETT!"

Saw one of my guys earlier today. Although every child is different, he really is one of the most unique children I've ever met. I was walking towards the building after talking to a student on his bus. Before I saw him, I heard his voice, and his one-of-a-kind way of occasionally greeting me, and it made my heart [and face] smile. As I've shared before[6], this is also the only student who routinely calls me Dr. Barrett; but sometimes he doesn't feel like it and it's totally cool with me. This is why a day without direct contact with a student is wasted.

[6]See May 6, 2019.

"ARE YOU GOING TO TAKE ME?"

Tested four students between 8:45 and 2:30 and wouldn't have it any other way. Much thanks to the teachers at Horizon Elementary School who made every student available when I came to their classrooms. And as an added bonus, a 4th grader asked me this after calling me Mr. Charles. It brought back nothing but the fondest memories of my days at Grove Park Elementary School in Baltimore when my students always called me Mr. Charles. And this, friends, is why a day without direct contact with students is wasted.

UNPROMPTED, UNSCRIPTED

"I love dubstep! I really like this! You have a lot of fun stuff in here. Can I flip the page? ...because your arm is probably hurting. I got it because I don't want your arm to hurt."

It's been a productive week evaluating students: four on Wednesday, one yesterday, and two today. Although it's far from everything that I do, I must say that I love this aspect of what I get to do every day: serve children, families, schools, and communities as a school psychologist! While testing a 3rd grade student yesterday morning, these were some of the things he said. None of these comments were prompted; but what was on his mind and he wanted to tell me. Thanks for being concerned about my arm, young man! I appreciate you offering to turn the pages.

"I DON'T KNOW.
WHEN I GET HOME, I'M GOING
TO RESEARCH THAT."

Children really don't know the wisdom that they possess. While evaluating a 4th grade student earlier this week, she made this profound statement in response to a Crystallized Intelligence question. For the second time this year, a child in elementary school illustrated that the essence of background knowledge is more appropriately an academic skill—factual information that can be taught or acquired—than an innate cognitive ability that predicts scholastic success. Listen to children. Children know. I wonder what they'll teach me tomorrow...

"IS HE YOUR FATHER?"

Today began with testing an absolutely brilliant and adorable 1st grader. And like many students whose complexion is similar to mine, at least one of her classmates asked, "Is he your father?" Although I've overheard this question many times over the past 12 years, today it led me to consider the following: if children can admit to seeing color, why don't we?

FROM ONE ANDREA
TO ANOTHER

Because children remember everything,
let's be sure to tell them things that are worth
remembering.

At 7:59 this morning, I was working with an absolutely delightful 3rd grader. And as I was getting my materials ready, she asked about a friend of mine who shared the same name. I remember telling her about Andrea Tse—a childhood friend whom I've known since 3rd grade—who is now a lawyer. I told her about Andrea because they pronounce their names the same way and it's important for children to know that there are people who look like them and have achieved great things. Although I didn't expect her to bring up this conversation, she did—and she was quite interested. She even remembered that Andrea had two children. This is why a day without direct contact with students is wasted.

MY. STUDENTS. ARE. AMAZING.

Most of the students I serve represent culturally and linguistically diverse backgrounds. And although some of their families/parents speak [some] English, a fair amount prefers to read in their native language, specifically Spanish. When evaluating students, for various reasons families aren't always able to attend meetings when their children are referred. As a result, I often send paper copies of behavior rating scales home with the student. Although I would rather not do this, at times it's the best (most efficient) option. Earlier today, a 4th grader returned a rating scale from her mother and I was convicted: am I contributing to the adultification of some students? Especially because students whose families don't speak or read English tend to also represent lower socioeconomic backgrounds, am I expecting more from these young people—burdening them with additional responsibilities—that I don't expect from their peers whose families speak English? To the young people who are forced to grow up prematurely, I see you and admire you. Although you shouldn't have to translate or interpret for your families, I see you and admire you. Although you shouldn't have to be the messenger—taking forms home and bringing them back, I see you and admire you. Because my students inspire me and teach me so much, this is why a day without direct contact with students is wasted.

A·SYN·CHRO·NOUS

The first meeting of the day was with the parents of a 1st grade boy who's actually age eligible for kindergarten. A very bright child, he is meeting the academic expectations of 1st grade. Behaviorally, however, he is experiencing some difficulties; working independently and remembering multi-step directions are particularly challenging. As we discussed interventions and ways to support the student, I wondered if we were expecting more from him than was developmentally appropriate. In other words, because he is doing well academically, doesn't mean that he is socially, emotionally, or behaviorally ready for 1st grade. Asynchronous simply means uneven. Whether you're raising children, or serving them as an educator, remember: sometimes the gift of time is what's best for children. And especially for children who are excelling academically, let's be sure that we're not rushing their development in other ways.

DO YOU HAVE ANY OTHER CLOTHES?

"Do you always wear suits every day?"

At 8:00 this morning, a 3rd grader asked me these questions. Why? I suppose he has an inquiring mind and wants to know. Because children are always looking at us and paying attention to things that we may not realize, let's be sure to give them something worth watching. And if you want to know the answers, please see below:

1. No.
2. Yes.

This is why a day without direct contact with students is wasted.

I DID IT!

"How am I going to do this? I did it!
Yes, I did it again!"

While writing a report for a 2nd grader I recently evaluated, I saw these notes in the margins of the test protocol (Differential Ability Scales, Second Edition). After she attempted the first item (Pattern Construction, #27), she was quite excited. And after she answered another one correctly, she was even more proud of herself.

Lesson #1: It's okay to talk to yourself.
Lesson #2: It's okay to encourage yourself.
Lesson #3: Success breeds success.
Lesson #4: Never overlook what's in the margins. Some of the most valuable perspective and insight can be found in the margins.

TESTING CHRONICLES

"Hi, nice beard."
Me: "Alright, last section." Student:
"And then I can go?
"We going?"
"What's your name?

The plan was to test five students. I was on track to meet my goal, but the last student was absent. I guess four out of five isn't too bad. The beard comment was made by a 5th grade student whom I did not know as he saw me walking in the hallway. Thanks! The others are humbling statements: maybe my games aren't as fun and engaging as I thought they were. We'll see what tomorrow brings: 'tis the season and two more are on deck.

THOSE ARE YOUR TOYS?

"Who dis?"

"I like your bracelet."

"Those are your toys? I thought you
meant video games."

"Why do you have a suitcase?"

"These are cool."

Well, today was a success! Met my goal
of testing two students and even got more than
halfway finished with the youngster who was absent
yesterday. I really should reconsider whether
describing my activities as games—especially when
they're in stimulus books—even with a 2nd grader,
is helpful or even believable. He did, however, think
that the blocks were cool. When I was getting the
second student, a peer asked her, "Who 'dis?" I
certainly wasn't expecting that! This was followed by
another curious student who had impeccable taste
(smile). Last, I guess a 1st grader thought that my
rolling briefcase looked as if I was heading to Gate
A27. And this, friends, is exactly why a day without
direct contact with students is wasted.

NONSENSE WORDS

"What's a...? Are you making these up?
'Cause these sound like nonsense words."

After testing seven students this week,
I spent a few hours scoring and catching up on
paperwork after the little darlings left for the day.
As I was scoring a subtest that assesses Crystallized
Intelligence (background knowledge), I saw these
words in the margin of the protocol. Said by a 2nd
grader, once again I was reminded of how insightful
children can be. And not only did it reinforce how
much background knowledge is both culturally and
linguistically loaded, it's probably better suited as
a measure of academic achievement rather than
cognitive ability. But for this youngster, in some ways
it also seemed to be nonsense. Hmmm...

MAKING UP WORDS

"What does... mean?" "I've never heard of that word,
so I don't know what it means."
"What is a...?"
"A unormous house." "I like your glasses."
"Please say this is going to be quick."

I must say: it's been a very productive few days of
testing three students. After testing seven last week,
I really hadn't planned on working with students
in this capacity; however, sometimes I simply can't
help it. And, a colleague convinced me to continue
getting ahead in case of a school closure. When I
went to get a student from his 5th grade classroom,
I realized something: I really work with children
who have impeccable taste (smile). Thanks for the
compliment on my glasses! Although the student
that I was picking up initially didn't seem too excited
about seeing me, he quickly warmed up and I think
he enjoyed himself. In addition to making up their
own words, children really have a gift for teaching
me things. Lesson: if children haven't been exposed
to words, they won't know what they mean. So...
why are we measuring Crystallized Intelligence as a
cognitive ability?

AUTHENTIC EQUITY

Sometimes the most authentic equity work doesn't include equity in its title or description because its inherently imbedded in its practices.

COVID-19 has certainly taught us, and continues to teach us, a lot about our practices as educators and education systems. As schools close for the safety and well-being of their students, families, staff, and larger community, finding creative ways to provide meaningful instructional experiences has been challenging. And because schools are also the source of meals for not only children but their families, this has presented its own set of opportunities to resolve. Although this global pandemic is an ever evolving and fluid situation, I appreciate the leaders of schools and school systems for how they are actively working towards promoting equitable outcomes for all students and families by continually refining their day-to-day practices. For example, having breakfast and lunches available for students to pick up from schools, although a good start, wasn't the most equitable practice as many students could not get to their schools. Therefore, delivering meals to where students are increases access and opportunity to truly benefit from what they need. And because instructional experiences will likely be online for the foreseeable future, ensuring that as many students as possible have the necessary devices and WIFI connectivity to continue their education is also a step in the right direction. Changing the structural practices and processes of how systems operate is the essence of socially just practices and fundamentally necessary to promote equitable outcomes for everyone.

A DAY WITHOUT DIRECT CONTACT WITH STUDENTS IS WASTED

It's been seven days since I've had direct contact with students. Although working for children and on behalf of children is important, I became a school psychologist to work with children.

IT'S COMPLICATED

As we're in the midst of one of the most significant events of our lifetimes, I continue to think about the implications for educating students. Scrolling through social media posts has shown me that there is no deficit of opinions about what schools should, and perhaps more importantly, should not be doing as many states have discontinued traditional instruction for the remainder of the 2019-2020 school year. And while I generally understand these diverse perspectives, I also want to offer the following: our opinions are likely informed by our own privilege or biased blind spots. Yes, families adjusting to distance learning is challenging while they're trying to manage the varied responsibilities of working (either at home or beyond), providing for their children, as well as the needs of loved ones. And because of this, in some ways, continuing education as if life is normal may not be the most pressing priority. But I also wonder: could it be that those who are suggesting that we don't focus on educating children have the ability to provide their children with the types of experiences that will make them less impacted when schools eventually reopen? Like many aspects of educating children, there is no easy answer or simple resolution to this conundrum. I am, however, suggesting that we think deeply about what really is best for children at this time. And because children and their families have such varied access to meaningful opportunities for their development, the answer really depends on individual circumstances. This, to me, is equity in education: not requiring all students to do the same thing but providing options that allow students to continue their academic development in the most effective and meaningful ways. Could some children afford to not engage in distance learning? Yes. But I also know that others cannot. And these young people, perhaps more than ever, require our most steadfast and unwavering support.

EQUITY IS PREVENTION

Promoting equitable outcomes for students includes establishing systems, processes, and structures that prevent disruption to the greatest extent possible. While all crises can't be anticipated or avoided, an equity framework ensures that socially just practices are infused into all aspects of school operations. As more and more schools are closing for the remainder of the school year, I continue to think about the lessons that we can learn from this significant event and the opportunities to fundamentally change the manner in which we not only serve students and families, but also prepare for their return.

IT COULD HAVE BEEN ME

       Extended school closures due to COVID-19 have led me to my own childhood. How would my family have weathered this storm? Throughout our time in Freeport Public Schools, my brothers and I were eligible to receive reduced priced lunch. I vividly remember paying $.25 each day. Although I never thought of it at the time, I guess we would have been considered students from a lower income background. It certainly never felt that way; my parents always made sure that we had everything we needed and many of the things that we wanted—private music lessons, participation in little league, school sports, yearly family vacations... But I also remember when they purchased our first computer. I was a sophomore or junior in high school. Yes, it was a very different time in history; but my brothers and I could have been students who needed a school issued device in order to access distance learning—one computer would simply not be enough for five children to share. And then I wonder how my parents would have managed to step into the role of teacher for five children while simultaneously providing for our most basic needs. This moment of transparency is meant to say that I see you—families juggling additional responsibilities with multiple children, students who may not have everything that they need to seamlessly access online instruction— and I understand. It could have been me in your shoes. Be encouraged. You can make it. You can succeed. You can accomplish more than you think.